Ripley's Believe It or Not!®

Developed and produced by Ripley Publishing Ltd

This edition published and distributed by:

Mason Crest
450 Parkway Drive, Suite D, Broomall, PA 19008
www.masoncrest.com

Printed and bound in the United States of America

First printing
9 8 7 6 5 4 3 2 1

Ripley's Believe It or Not!
Seriously Weird!
ISBN: 978-1-4222-3142-5 (hardback)
Ripley's Believe It or Not!—Complete 8 Title Series
ISBN: 978-1-4222-3138-8

Cataloging-in-Publication Data is on file with the Library of Congress

PUBLISHER'S NOTE
While every effort has been made to verify the accuracy of the entries in this book, the
Publishers cannot be held responsible for any errors contained in the work. They would
be glad to receive any information from readers.

WARNING
Some of the stunts and activities in this book are undertaken by experts and should not
be attempted by anyone without adequate training and supervision.

Ripley's Believe It or Not!

Dare To Look

SERIOUSLY WEIRD!

www.MasonCrest.com

SERIOUSLY WEIRD!

Incredibly Strange. Open up your eyes to a world of fantastic feats, amazing tales, and sensational stories. Read about the portraits made from meat, the man with elastic skin, and the lickable wallpaper!

This squirrel became trapped in a drain in the middle of the road, but after managing to poke its head out it was spotted and freed...

YOUR UPLOADS

BOUND TO SUCCEED▶
Ana Lominadze, a 17-year-old Georgian schoolgirl, swam a 6,000-yd (5,500-m) stretch of the Dardanelles, a narrow strait in Turkey, in 50 minutes on August 30, 2012—with her hands and legs bound! The style of swimming, with tied hands and feet, is known as Colchian and is traditional in Georgia, where it is used for military training. Ana not only broke the world record for swimming across the Dardanelles Colchian-style, she also became the first woman to complete the crossing by that method.

CHANCE FIND▶ Jesse Matos of Mount Shasta, California, lost his high-school class ring when he accidentally flushed it down the toilet in 1938—and it was found 73 years later in a sewer by sanitation worker Tony Congi, who graduated from the same high school in 1976 and recognized the ring immediately.

NOT ETHICAL▶ A man was charged with stealing a book on ethics from the University of Louisville, Kentucky, and then trying to sell it to a college bookstore in the city.

FAMILY DAY▶ Stefanie Thomas and her husband Paul of Plymouth, England, both have birthdays on September 6—and when their first child, Oliver, was born in 2011, it was also on September 6!

HUMAN DOORSTOP▶ A would-be burglar was arrested in Brockton, Massachusetts, after his head got stuck under a garage door for nine hours. He had tried to prop open the heavy roll-up door with a piece of metal, but it slipped and the falling door pinned his head against the concrete floor until he was discovered the following morning.

HAIR RISK▶ Hair Grooming Syncope is a pediatric disorder that results in a child suffering fainting spells whenever his or her hair is brushed or cut.

SPIDER TERROR▶ An entire office building in Chur, Switzerland, was evacuated in July 2012 over a plastic spider. Workers panicked after seeing the lifelike creature on the boss's desk, but when police officers arrived they quickly discovered that the giant bird-eating spider was a fake.

DISTANT TWINS▶ Reuben and Floren Blake of Gloucestershire, England, are twins, but they were born five years apart. They were conceived from the same batch of embryos during fertility treatment, but after the birth of Reuben in 2006, the remaining three embryos were frozen until his parents, Simon and Jody Blake, were ready to try for another child.

BEACH BOTTLE▶ On the Baltic Sea coast near Kaliningrad, Daniil Korotkikh, a 13-year-old Russian boy, found a message in a bottle that had been written 24 years earlier by a then five-year-old German boy, Frank Uesbeck.

TIDY SUM▶ Nagged for weeks by his mother to tidy up his bedroom, 19-year-old Ryan Kitching of Midlothian, Scotland, finally gave in to her wishes—and in a pile of papers in a drawer he found a £53,000 ($83,600) winning lottery ticket.

YODA COIN▶ In 2011, the Pacific island nation of Niue released legal tender coins featuring *Star Wars* characters, including Luke Skywalker, Princess Leia, and Yoda. Queen Elizabeth II appears on the reverse of the coins, which were issued by the New Zealand mint.

ROBOT GUARDS▶ Scientists in South Korea have developed robot guards to patrol the country's prisons. The 5-ft-tall (1.5-m) robots run on four wheels and are fitted with sensors, which enable them to detect abnormal behavior among prisoners and then report it to the officers in charge.

SNAKE ATTACK▶ A man who stopped to withdraw money from an ATM in Alava, Spain, got more than he bargained for when a snake slithered out of the machine and tried to attack him. The snake had somehow become trapped in the cash-point mechanism.

SLEEPY SWIMMER▶ Alyson Bair of Burley, Idaho, twice went swimming in the nearby Snake River—while sleepwalking. On the first occasion she dreamed she was drowning, only to wake up in the river, and the second time she was found soaking wet a quarter of a mile downstream from her home.

BRAZILIAN BATMAN▶ In 2012, city officials in Taubaté, Brazil, hired former soldier André Luiz Pinheiro to dress up as Batman and patrol the streets of the most crime-ridden neighborhoods.

SMART BED▶ A Spanish furniture company has invented an electronic bed that makes itself. Three seconds after the last person gets out of the bed, mechanical arms automatically grab the edges of the duvet, rollers smooth down the sheets, and a set of levers straightens the pillows.

GOOD HAIR DAY

3 ft 8 in (1.1 m) high!

PRICELESS DOORSTOP▶ A blue-and-white Ming Dynasty ceramic vase, which had been used as a doorstop by a family in Long Island, New York, was sold at an auction in 2012 for $1.3 million. The family realized the value of their doorstop only when they saw a similar piece advertised for sale in an auction house catalogue.

RADIO REVELATION▶ The elements americium and curium, discovered during the United States' top-secret nuclear bomb project, were first announced on a 1945 edition of a children's radio quiz show, *Quiz Kids*, even before they were presented to the scientific community.

FLASH MOB▶ Jack Cushman from Boston, Massachusetts, proposed to his girlfriend Teresa Elsey by organizing a flash mob involving hundreds of complete strangers. He arranged for up to 300 people to approach her in the street as they were walking together and each hand her a single carnation. While she was surrounded, he slipped away, changed into a tuxedo, and returned with a microphone to propose.

MOUNTAINTOP CEREMONY▶ Avid climbers Bob Ewing and his bride Antonie Hodge Ewing got married on the narrow summit of a 900-ft-high (274-m) mountain in West Virginia. The groom made the sheer ascent of Seneca Rocks in a tuxedo while the bride accessorized her mother's wedding gown with a helmet and hiking shoes. Her mother Evangeline, a novice climber, also made it to the top to witness the happy event.

▶ Designer Kazuhiro Watanabe from Tokyo, Japan, has a spire-like Mohawk haircut that is an incredible 3 ft 8 in (1.1 m) high. He has been growing it for more than 15 years and it takes stylists two hours plus three cans of hairspray and a large bottle of gel to extend it to its maximum height.

SALT POOL

▶ A giant, 323,000-sq-ft (30,000-sq-m) swimming pool in Sichuan Province, China, can hold up to 10,000 bathers at a time. The man-made saltwater pool, known as China's Dead Sea, was created using the area's wealth of salt resources and contains 43 different minerals and microelements.

TELLTALE TATTOO▶ In 2011, police in Colorado captured 60-year-old Frederick Barrett 32 years after he had escaped from jail in Florida. After all that time, they were able to identify him by a tattoo of a cross and a dot on his right hand.

UNBEATABLE ROBOT▶ Scientists at the University of Tokyo, Japan, have devised a robot that is unbeatable at the game of Rock, Paper, Scissors. By using advanced motion-sensing technology, the robot needs just a millisecond to recognize the position and shape of a human hand and can therefore detect in advance what hand-shape its opponent is about to choose.

OCEAN ORDEAL▶ Nineteen-year-old Ryan Harris spent 26 hours adrift in a small plastic fishing crate in the icy waters off the coast of Alaska after being washed overboard. When his boat was sunk by huge waves, Harris, from nearby Sitka, spent the night in the crate, which measured just 4 x 4 ft (1.2 x 1.2 m), before finally being rescued by a coastguard helicopter. He kept his spirits up by singing and survived with nothing worse than a cut head and blisters from gripping the crate.

LUCKY ERROR▶ Richard Brown of Taunton, Massachusetts, was given the wrong scratch-off lottery ticket by a distracted store clerk—but he didn't complain and won $1 million.

MARRIED RESCUER▶ An avalanche survivor married the mountain rescue guide who had saved her life two years earlier—and the ceremony took place 6,000 ft (1,800 m) up on the very mountain where she was almost swept to her death. Tatjana Rasevic was buried under tons of snow on Serbia's Suva Planina mountain range until Nenad Podova dug her out.

▶ Sideshow performer James Morris could stretch his skin as much as 18 in (46 cm) from his body and could pull the skin of his neck over his head so that it looked like an elephant's trunk. He was also able to pull the skin of one leg and cover the other leg with it. Morris was born in Copenhagen, New York, in 1859 without the interior third layer of skin on his body. As a result, his skin was not bound to the flesh beneath, permitting him to stretch and pull it in any direction. A barber by trade, he used his unique talent to amuse friends and coworkers and began to perform at the dime museum of J.E. Sackett in Providence, Rhode Island. In 1882, he joined the legendary Barnum & Bailey Circus earning $150 a week, and toured the world with them to great acclaim, billed as either "The Elastic Man" or "The India Rubber Man."

ELASTIC MAN

POTTY IDEA

▶ *You need a head for heights to use the toilet in this luxury penthouse in Guadalajara, Mexico—because it is suspended on a glass floor above a 15-story abandoned elevator shaft. When you sit on the toilet or brush your teeth, you can look straight through the floor to the bottom of the shaft.*

PHOTO SHOCK▶ Addison Logan, 13, bought an old Polaroid camera for $1 at a Wichita, Kansas, garage sale—and inside he found a photograph of a dead uncle he had never met.

SLIM CHANCE▶ George McCovery of West Palm Beach, Florida, had his jail sentence cut short by a judge in 2011 after he met a court-sanctioned weight challenge and dropped 25 lb (11 kg) in only 20 days.

LOVE LETTER▶ In July 2011, Muhammad Siddeeq of Indianapolis, Indiana, received a love letter that had been mailed to him 53 years earlier. Since then he had married twice—once to the letter writer—fathered 21 children, and changed his name.

SALMON CROSSING▶ After a river flooded in Mason County, Washington, dozens of salmon were seen trying to swim across an adjacent road. Cars were not their only problem, with at least one unlucky salmon being snapped up by a passing dog.

CHRISTMAS TREES▶ Brandon Smith and Dennis Guyette decorated their home in Greenwood, Indiana, with 68 Christmas trees—and their decorations adorned every room, including the bathroom and kitchen. When they opened their festive house to the public, they had more than 600 visitors.

TOY STORY▶ After a miaowing sound was heard coming from a locked recycling container in Anglesey, Wales, fire crews and animal rescuers tried in vain to gain entry. Eventually the container was loaded onto a truck and driven 20 mi (32 km) to a specialist engineering firm, where steel saws forced it open and revealed the trapped cat in fact to be a lifelike, miaowing Disney toy of Marie the cat from *The Aristocats* movie.

MILITARY FORESIGHT▶ In the 1917 Battle of Messines of World War I, 10,000 German soldiers were instantly killed by 500 tons of explosives that had been planted underground by Allied engineers who had anticipated the battle a year earlier!

LIGHTEST MATERIAL▶ Scientific researchers in California have created the world's lightest material—one that is 99.9 percent air. Made of tiny hollow metallic tubes arranged into a micro-lattice, it is 100 times lighter than Styrofoam. In fact, it is so light that it can sit on top of dandelion fluff without damaging it.

HIGHWAY BIRTHS▶ On July 28, 2012, Siobhan Anderson from Amityville, New York, gave birth to twins on two different highways while on her way to the hospital. After going into labor a week early, she gave birth to Gavin on the Southern State Parkway in Long Island and 11 minutes later to Declan on Wantagh State Parkway.

ENGINE ATTACK▶ An 11½-ft-long (3.5-m) saltwater crocodile jumped out of the water and bit chunks out of a boat's engine during a 90-minute nighttime attack in Australia's South Alligator River. The moored boat's three occupants eventually fought off the croc by smacking it over the head with a metal pole.

ISLAND RESCUE▶ Setting off in a canoe in Wild Fowl Bay, Michigan, Nathan Bluestein carried out an elaborate, meticulously planned marriage proposal to May Gorial, but the couple then had to be rescued by sheriff's deputies after severe weather left them stranded on a nearby island.

DIRTY DISHES▶ Customers at a French restaurant in Tokyo, Japan, pay $110 to eat dirt. Toshio Tanabe, chef at Ne Quittez Pas, devised the dirt menu after winning a cooking contest with his earthy sauce. He uses a special black soil that has been tested for safety and then serves up such delights as potato starch and black dirt soup, followed by a vegetable salad with a black dirt dressing, sea bass with a dirt risotto, dirt ice cream, and finally dirt mint tea.

CUPCAKE MOSAIC▶ To celebrate Singapore's 47th birthday, 1,200 youth volunteers created a mosaic—in the shape of a pair of hands around the national flag—from 20,000 cupcakes. The mosaic measured 52 x 26 ft (15.8 x 7.9 m), and was made from 1,320 lb (600 kg) of cupcake mix, 770 lb (350 kg) of eggs, and 660 lb (300 kg) of vegetable oil. It required 16 decks of ovens and more than 18 hours of baking.

$900 BEER▶ A single bottle of Samuel Adams Utopias, a dark beer brewed by the Boston Beer Company of Massachusetts, was sold on eBay for a staggering $900 in 2013. Sold in a ceramic bottle, the beer has high alcohol content and is aged for up to 20 years in a variety of casks. Only a limited number of bottles are released each year.

BAT FLAKES▶ A German man was horrified when he poured out a bowl of cornflakes for breakfast—and found a mummified bat in the pack. Experts in Stuttgart believe the bat had flown into the packaging by mistake and had suffocated to death.

MONSTER PIZZA▶ Big Mama's and Papa's Pizzeria of Los Angeles, California, offers the world's largest deliverable pizza—a monster pie measuring 54 x 54 in (1.35 x 1.35 m). It costs $200, feeds up to 70 people, and is so big it has to be delivered in truck beds and maneuvered through doorways.

TALLEST CAKE▶ At Luoyang, China, in March 2012, a total of 20 chefs spent more than 24 hours perched on scaffolding to make a giant cake that weighed nearly 4,400 lb (2,000 kg) and stood a staggering 26 ft 2 in (8 m) tall. The eight-tiered cake, which was held in place by metal plates to prevent it from toppling over, required 1,100 lb (500 kg) of eggs, 572 lb (260 kg) of flour, 440 lb (200 kg) of cream, 220 lb (100 kg) of fruit, and 176 lb (80 kg) of chocolate.

BULLY BEER▶ After announcing that it was making beer from bull testicles as an April Fool's Day joke, the Wynkoop Brewing Company of Denver, Colorado, received such a positive response to the idea that it decided to produce the beer for real. Taking the local name for fried bull's testicles—a delicacy in Colorado—Rocky Mountain Oyster Stout has a dark brown color with flavors of chocolate syrup and espresso.

WHISKY GALORE▶ Czech glassmakers blew by hand the world's biggest whisky bottle to meet an order from Glenturret, one of Scotland's oldest whisky distilleries, as part of its 107-year anniversary celebrations. Standing 5 ft 5 in (1.6 m) tall and weighing 110 lb (50 kg), the 482-pt (228-l) bottle took three hours to fill with Glenturret's whisky. It went on display in August 2012 at the Glenturret visitor center, which annually welcomes more than 200,000 whisky lovers.

WATER BUGS
▶ Food shoppers at Tung Kwian market in northern Thailand can buy a traditional local dish of water bugs. Their legs tied up with green string, the insects are sold alive so that they stay fresh before being fried.

LICKABLE WALLPAPER

▶ *Wallpaper featuring 1,325 lickable chocolate and orange Jaffa cake-flavored stickers was pasted on to an elevator at a communications firm in London, England. Inspired by the movie* Willy Wonka & the Chocolate Factory, *the art installation, called* Spot of Jaffa, *was inspired by chef Heston Blumenthal and artist Damien Hirst. To prevent the spread of germs, each sticker could be licked only once before an attendant removed it and replaced it with a fresh one.*

GOLD CUPCAKE▶ Made from the finest chocolate and coated in edible 23-carat gold sheets, the Golden Phoenix cupcake went on sale in Dubai for a staggering $1,010, making it the world's most expensive cupcake.

POTATO PILE▶ A hefty 92,500 lb (42,000 kg) of locally grown potatoes were arranged in nearly 10,000 bags at Sobeys store in Charlottetown, Prince Edward Island, Canada, on October 3, 2012, to form a gigantic potato display.

NAAN BREAD▶ Using a 20-ft-wide (6-m) oven, volunteers in Xinjiang, China, took ten hours to bake a giant naan bread 9 ft (2.7 m) in diameter and stuffed with meat dumplings. It included 66 lb (30 kg) of mutton, 275 lb (125 kg) of flour, and 35 lb (16 kg) of onion.

MAKIN' BACON▶ Farmer Huang Demin from Hunan Province, China, has built a 10-ft (3-m) wooden diving board for his pigs to jump off because he says it makes their meat taste better. Since his pigs have been diving headfirst into a pond each day, he has been able to charge three times the price of normal pork for their meat.

HORSE SAUSAGE▶ Chefs in Xinjiang, China, used meat from 38 horses to make a 700-ft-long (213-m) sausage weighing 2,769 lb (1,256 kg).

TORTA TREAT▶ Over 50 cooks in Mexico City prepared a 173-ft-long (53-m), 1,540-lb (700-kg) torta sandwich made from 70 different ingredients, including thousands of pieces of bread, lettuce, onion, and tomato and hundreds of pints of mayo, mustard, and spicy sauces.

CRAB CAKE▶ At the 2012 Maryland State Fair, cooks made a 300-lb (136-kg) crab cake from around 1,600 crabs. They used 200 lb (90 kg) of crabmeat, and eggs, breadcrumbs, and seasoning.

OPOSSUM-SPIT COFFEE▶ A coffee plantation in Pedra Azul, Brazil, is charging $450 for a kilo (2.2 lb) of exclusive coffee beans that have been chewed by a gray four-eyed opossum, or cuica. Plantation owner Rogério Lemke observed the marsupials eating the shell and sweet sticky substance that surrounds the coffee bean but spitting out most of the bean itself. Tests showed that the animals selected only the best fruit, so the beans they spat out were the cream of the crop.

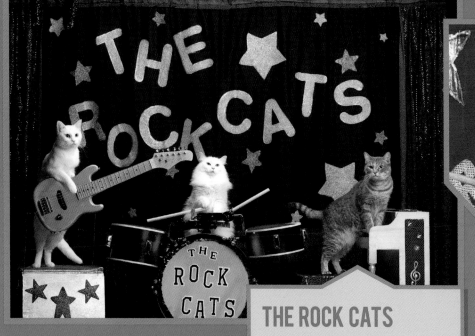

THE ROCK CATS

▶ Believe it or not, this is a real band called The Rock Cats! They are real cats that play real instruments! Samantha Martin from Austin, Texas, has been training the animals since she was nine years old, and uses her own pets.

BRIDE'S POTATO▶ A potato variety known as the Bride's Potato gets its name from an Inca practice of requiring a bride to peel potatoes to prove her skills as a good wife.

EXTRA LEGS▶ A woman from Changsha, China, freaked out when she got home and realized that the frozen chicken she had bought from a supermarket had four legs!

MEATY MOUTHFUL▶ For the 2012 launch of reality TV show *Man vs. Food Nation* on Food Network U.K , chef Tristan Welch created a sandwich filled with 40 different cuts of meat. Standing 14 in (35 cm) high and 24 in (60 cm) wide, the sandwich took four hours to make and weighed about 28 lb (12.7 kg). It contained 11 lb (5 kg) of meat, including salami, turkey, bacon, ham, sausage, and chorizo.

PANCAKE STACK▶ On February 21, 2012—Shrove Tuesday—chef Andy Wrobel built a 30-in-high (76-cm) stack of 60 pancakes in Melbourne, Australia. He flips over 100,000 pancakes every year at the restaurant where he has worked for more than 25 years.

BURGER PIZZA▶ In 2012, Pizza Hut launched its Crown Crust Burger pizza in the Middle East—a pizza crust lined with a dozen cheeseburgers.

CAT CAFÉ▶ In a bid to introduce Japanese culture to Vienna, Austria, Takako Ishimitsu has opened the Café Neko, a cat café where customers can play with five resident cats while enjoying their coffee. There are around 40 cat cafés in Tokyo, Japan, where they are very popular.

STILL EDIBLE▶ Hans Feldmeier of Rostock, Germany, received a tin of lard in 1948 from a U.S. food-aid program and finally decided to eat the 64-year-old contents in 2012.

PAPER BOTTLE▶ Martin Myerscough from Suffolk, England, has invented the world's first paper wine bottle. The bottle combines a paper outer casing with a thin plastic lining to keep the wine fresh.

LARGEST LASAGNA▶ On June 20, 2012, chefs in Krakow, Poland, made the world's biggest lasagna, weighing more than an adult African elephant. Tipping the scales at 15,697 lb (7,120 kg), the lasagna took ten hours to bake before being sliced into 10,000 portions. It was made in support of the Italian soccer team who were based in the city for the Euro 2012 soccer championships.

STUCK ON YOU

▶ For nearly 20 years, people have been sticking pieces of chewing gum to a 50-ft-long (15-m) brick wall in Seattle, Washington, so that the sticky deposits are now several inches thick in places. At first, they used the gum to stick coins to the wall in Post Alley, but now it's just gum. Newlyweds have even chosen the gum wall as a backdrop for their wedding pictures, and it was also featured briefly in the 2009 Jennifer Aniston movie, *Love Happens*.

FLOWER POWER

▶ Believe it or not, these sculptures are made entirely from flowers! On the first Sunday of every September, the Bloemencorso, or flower parade, makes its way through the streets of the Dutch town of Zundert, the birthplace of artist Vincent van Gogh. Hundreds of volunteers pin specially grown dahlias to wire frames to create each float.

FAKE FAMILY

▶ *Alice Winstone from Cardigan, Wales, has spent nearly $20,000 creating a nursery for 50 fake babies who share the house with three of her five real children. Unable to have any more children of her own, she has instead filled the house with lifelike reborn dolls, buying them racks of designer clothes, cots, and strollers, and even taking her favorites out for day trips in the car. She feeds, changes, washes, and sleeps with her dolls, which all proved too much for her husband who moved out over five years ago. She says: "I look after the dolls like I would my own babies—they are so lifelike and I feel such a close bond with them. It's the best of both worlds as well—I get to dress them up, do their hair, and wash their clothes without the endless dirty nappies and sleepless nights!"*

Costing between $75 and $4,000 each, reborn dolls take the place of real babies for some parents who even buy fake birth or adoption certificates for them. First appearing in the United States in the early 1990s, a reborn doll is created by adding layers of paint and other features to an ordinary vinyl doll in order to make it look like a genuine baby. Veins can be painted on for an authentic newborn look, while the arms and head are often weighted with sand or rubber pellets for a more realistic feel. Buyers can request made-to-order features on the doll, such as an umbilical cord, baby fat, human hair, particular color eyes, or a magnet inserted inside the mouth for attaching a pacifier. Some reborn dolls can be "fed" a fake form of milk and even be fitted with mechanisms that simulate breathing to make it appear that the doll is alive. In 2008, police in Queensland, Australia, smashed a car window to rescue what appeared to be an unconscious baby, only to find it was a reborn doll.

TREASURE TROVE▶ After hunting in vain for buried treasure in the same area of Jersey in the Channel Islands for 30 years, amateur metal detectors Reg Mead and Richard Miles finally hit the jackpot when they unearthed three-quarters of a ton of Iron Age coins worth $15 million. Each of the 50,000 or so 2,000-year-old silver coins they dug up—the largest-ever haul of Celtic coins—has an estimated value of $300.

CROSSED WIRES▶ A woman from Zlin, Czech Republic, had to be rescued after mistaking an electrical pylon for a bridge. She climbed the 40-ft-high (12-m) pylon in the belief that it would take her across the Morava River.

PLASTIC ARM▶ Part of the M62 motorway in Merseyside, England, was closed by police for hours because of a plastic arm. The false limb, lying in the middle of the road, caused chaos after drivers mistook it for a genuine human arm.

FIRST GIRL▶ In 2011, Gary and Satish Beckett of Kent, England, celebrated the birth of daughter Anaia—the first girl to be born into the family for 113 years.

UNLUCKY DAY▶ A man got stuck in an elevator twice in one day. After being trapped for three hours on the 21st floor of Chicago's Mid-Continental Plaza on February 6, 2012, he was finally freed by fire crews. Moments later he took another elevator down, but that became stuck, too!

LOTTERY SCOOP▶ New Taipei City, Taiwan, cleaned up its streets by offering lottery tickets to people who cleared up dog poop. More than 4,000 people collected 14,500 bags of excrement over a four-month period—and each bag was rewarded with a ticket.

KNIT WIT ▶ This plate of fish, fries, peas, and two slices of lemon looks good enough to eat—but in fact the entire meal is made from yarn! Artistic knitter Kate Jenkins from Brighton, England, spends hours with a crochet hook to create a whole menu of amusing, edible-looking designs—including bottles of wine, ketchup, cans of soup, and fruit-topped pastries—sometimes embroidering patterns on to her tasty creations for added realism.

BUSY BIRTHDAY ▶ Sammy Kellett of Lancashire, England, has three sons, Keiran, Kaiden, and Kyle, all of whom were born on September 20—in 2005, 2008, and 2011—at odds of 133,590 to one.

COVERS BLESSED ▶ Priests in Lodz, Poland, blessed all 4,000 of the town's manhole covers to try to stop scrap metal thieves stealing them.

HUNTER HUNTED ▶ A man who went duck hunting on the Great Salt Lake, Utah, was hospitalized after his dog stepped on a shotgun, shooting him in the butt.

HEAVY READING ▶ The *Earth Platinum* atlas weighed 330 lb (150 kg)—each page measuring 6 ft (1.8 m) high and 4 ft 6 in (1.4 m) wide.

TWO CRASHES ▶ On March 13, 2012, mother Annie Price and her son Antony O'Halloran survived separate head-on crashes within four minutes of each other on New Zealand's Kapiti Coast.

RING RECOVERED ▶ Sixteen years after losing her wedding ring, farmer's wife Lena Paahlsson of Mora, Sweden, found it wrapped around a carrot in her garden. She had taken off the ring while cooking in 1995 and thinks it must have fallen into the kitchen sink and become mixed up with potato peelings that were composted or fed to the farm's sheep—all her garden soil comes from either composted vegetables or sheep dung.

GOLD TRAIL ▶ When termites encounter a gold vein, they bore through it and deposit the displaced gold outside their hive. In Mali, miners use the termites' geological discoveries to plan new gold hunting expeditions.

EVIL CLOWN

▶ *Swiss actor Dominic Deville hires himself out as an evil clown who stalks and terrifies children in the week leading up to their birthday. He sends them scary texts, makes prank phone calls and, finally, when they are least expecting it, he splats a cake in their face. Deville, who came up with the idea from watching horror movies, says kids love being scared senseless, but promises that if the parents become concerned, he will back off.*

SAY CHEESE!

▶ Artist Jason Baalman created portraits of 2012 U.S. presidential candidates Barack Obama and Mitt Romney from more than 2,000 Cheetos. Jason from Colorado Springs, Colorado, spent over 100 hours carefully positioning and gluing the cheese-flavored snacks onto a black canvas to create an edible artwork measuring 3 x 4 ft (0.9 x 1.2 m). Jason, who has also used ketchup and barbecue sauce in his pictures, has previously made Cheetos portraits of talk-show host Conan O'Brien and singer Cee Lo Green.

LOOK-ALIKE NUGGET▶ Rebekah Speight of Dakota City, Nebraska, sold a three-year-old McDonald's Chicken McNugget that resembled the profile of George Washington for $8,100 on eBay

SPAGHETTI STRUCTURE▶ Students in Iran used 100,000 ft (33,000 m) of spaghetti—that's over 20 mi (33 km)—to build a gridlike structure that measured 79 ft (24 m) long, 16 ft (5 m) tall, and 18 ft (5.5 m) wide and weighed 226 lb (103 kg). It took them two months to make.

PARTY PIE▶ For a 2012 St. Patrick's Day party, chefs in Wildwood, New Jersey, created a 1,805-lb (819-kg) meat and potato pie, made up of 880 lb (400 kg) of minced beef, 775 lb (352 kg) of potatoes, 110 lb (50 kg) of carrots, and 100 lb (45 kg) of onions.

ROYAL LANDLORD▶ In keeping with a 500-year-old tradition, the landlord of the Ship Inn on the half-mile-long Piel Island off the northwest coast of England is entitled to call himself the King of Piel.

OWL CURRY▶ For more than 30 years, the only meat that taxidermist Jonathan McGowan of Bournemouth, England, has eaten has been roadkill—including such dishes as owl curry, rat stir-fry, adder in butter, badger stew, and squirrel pie. He first developed a taste for roadkill at age 14 after cooking a dead adder snake that he had discovered and deciding it tasted like bacon rind. He says squirrels ("like rabbit, but not as overpowering"), foxes ("lean and never any fat"), and rats ("like pork but quite salty") are particularly delicious, but he is not as keen on mice ("very bitter"), hedgehogs ("all fatty meat"), and moles ("horrible with a rancid taste").

PAPER SNACKS▶ Ann Curran of Dundee, Scotland, has developed a taste for eating her local newspaper. She says the Dundee *Evening Telegraph* is the "only newsprint with the proper flavor" and keeps shredded copies in her handbag for when she feels like a snack.

MARSHMALLOW ROAST▶ On March 24, 2012, 1,272 people gathered at Marion, Kansas, to roast marshmallows simultaneously around a giant bonfire that was 660 ft (201 m) long, 6 ft (1.8 m) wide, and 3 ft (0.9 m) tall.

ROOF FLOCK▶ Wei Xingyu keeps a small flock of sheep on the roof of his four-story house in Changsha, China, so that his baby daughter has a regular supply of fresh milk. He has put down grass for his sheep to graze on, and if they get too hot on the roof, he walks them to his parents' house.

LIZARD FILLING

▶ Ian Lock from Derbyshire, England, was horrified to find this 6-in (15-cm) lizard crawling in a bag of supermarket wild arugula salad from Italy as he was about to make a sandwich.

YOUR UPLOADS

EGGSTRAORDINARY!
▶ Ripley's were sent this picture by Josh Scott from Corbin, Kentucky, showing him holding an unbelievable 21 eggs in one hand!

KILLER COCKTAIL▶ Nick Nicora made a 10,500-gal (32,176-l) margarita cocktail at the 2012 California State Fair in Sacramento. The drink was poured into a 25-ft-tall (7.6-m), 20-horsepower blender.

BEER TRAIN▶ Instead of using waiters, the Vytopna Restaurant in Prague, Czech Republic, delivers drinks to its customers on a 1,300-ft-long (396-m) model railroad that runs through the restaurant building.

GASSY DISHES▶ As well as serving food as a solid or a liquid, the Juniper Kitchen and Wine Bar in Ottawa, Ontario, serves it as a calorie-free gas to be inhaled by the customer. Liquid-based foods such as soups are poured into a device called Le Whaf, a large glass cylinder with an ultrasound attached. The ultrasound agitates the mix, creating a vapor cloud that is filled with the flavor of the soup, but without any of the calories.

RECORD ROLL▶ A group of 285 chefs cooked a 1,525-ft-long (465-m) fried spring roll in Semarang, Indonesia—that's more than a quarter of a mile long! It needed an incredible 2,156 lb (980 kg) of bamboo shoots and 15,000 spring roll skins, as well as five frying pans, to create the whopper.

CAN OPENER▶ British merchant Peter Durand invented the tin can in 1810, but it was not until 1858 that Ezra Warner of Waterbury, Connecticut, invented the can opener! Before that, cans had to be hammered open.

POOP TEA▶ Businessman An Yanshi from Sichuan, China, purchased 11 tons of poop from a giant panda breeding center—and used it to make the world's most expensive tea, selling for over $200 a cup. He says his panda dung tea is special because the animals absorb only a fraction of the nutrients in their food—70 percent of the nutrients are passed in their feces.

DOUBLE EGG▶ Sean Wilson from Hampshire, England, was surprised when his hen Rosie laid a colossal egg that weighed 6.4 oz (181 g), and was even more amazed when he cracked the egg open and found another egg shell inside! The "rare egg inside an egg" video quickly became an online sensation with 500,000 views in a week.

ONE-TON PUMPKIN▶ Ron Wallace of Greene, Rhode Island, grew the world's first one-ton pumpkin, and his 2,009-lb (911-kg) giant, nicknamed "The Freak II" earned him more than $15,000 when he exhibited it at the 2012 Topsfield Fair in Massachusetts. His record-breaking pumpkin reached that weight in just one growing season, starting from a single tiny seed.

SPACE BURGER▶ Five students from Harvard University, Massachusetts, launched a burger nearly 100,000 ft (30,000 m) into space tied to a helium balloon. Using an attached camera, they filmed it soaring where no burger has ever gone before until the balloon burst and the burger fell back to Earth, landing in a tree outside Boston.

SUPER SAUSAGE▶ Ptacek's IGA grocery store of Prescott, Wisconsin, celebrated its centenary on October 6, 2012, by making a 52-ft-2-in-long (16-m) bratwurst. The super sausage, which slotted into a bun made from 40 lb (18 kg) of dough, was so big that it took a dozen people to turn it every few minutes while it was grilling.

EDIBLE QUEEN▶ Food artist Michelle Wibowo from Brighton, England, made a life-size sculpture weighing 55 lb (25 kg) of Queen Elizabeth II fashioned from sugar paste, accompanied by a royal corgi dog made from fruitcake.

BLOOD FEAST

▶Fifty guests at the Livingston Restaurant in Atlanta, Georgia, paid $85 each to eat eight blood-inspired dishes. Masterminded by head chef Zeb Stevenson, the special Blood Dinner menu included currant bread mixed with bacon and pork blood and served with bone marrow butter, smoked eel in an eel blood broth, blood sausage and, for dessert, pomegranate and pork blood-enriched crème anglaise (pictured here) drizzled into liquid nitrogen.

STICKY FINGERS ▶ Scientists at England's University of Leicester say that criminals with a taste for fast food run a greater risk of being caught. The creators of a new forensic fingerprint say people who eat foods with a high salt content have "sticky fingers," which are more likely to leave a telltale mark at a crime scene.

BLIND FAITH ▶ Vietnamese cook Christine Ha won the 2012 series of Fox's *MasterChef*—even though she is blind. Suffering from an autoimmune disorder that affects the optic nerves, she lost sight in one eye in 1999 and was completely blind by 2007, but uses her heightened sense of smell and taste to compensate for her lack of vision. She has spent years re-creating her mother's favorite recipes, purely by taste.

LONGEST PARSNIP ▶ In 2012, Peter Glazebrook from Nottinghamshire, England, grew a record-breaking parsnip that was an incredible 18 ft 6 in (5.6 m) long—36 times the length of a normal parsnip. He has previously held the record for the longest beet at 21 ft (6.4 m), and the largest potato at 8 lb 4 oz (3.7 kg).

TOP DOG ▶ At Little Rock, Arkansas, in May 2012, vendor "Hot Dog Mike" Juliano sold four hot dogs for charity, each costing a whopping $1,501. TheONEdog was made up of lobster tails, gold flakes, saffron, and high-quality beef.

SPACE LETTUCE ▶ Mizuna lettuce was the first plant to grow in space successfully through two generations—aboard the *Mir* Space Station.

MOUSE BACON ▶ Wan Shen's butcher's shop in Guangdong Province, China, sells nothing but freshly caught, free-range mice, a dish considered so tasty by locals that pound for pound it is more expensive than chicken or pork. Among Wan Shen's specialties is cured mouse bacon, where the rodent is delicately carved into tiny slices.

CAKE PORTRAIT ▶ To mark the Diamond Jubilee of Queen Elizabeth II in 2012, German-born baker Gerhard Jenne created a portrait of the Queen from 3,120 individually colored, frosted cakes—one for every week of her reign. It contained around 1,000 eggs, 200 packets of butter, 150 bags of sugar, and 79 lb (36 kg) of marzipan.

SUNDAE BEST ▶ On May 6, 2012, at Lake Forest, California, some 400 volunteers built the world's longest ice-cream sundae, measuring a whopping 222 ft 9¾ in (67.9 m).

CHOCOLATE NATION ▶ Germans are the world's most enthusiastic chocolate eaters, consuming an average of 25 lb (11.3 kg) of chocolate per person every year.

TEMPTING FATE ▶ On February 11, 2012, a man suffered a heart attack while eating a 6,000-calorie Triple By-Pass Burger at the Heart Attack Grill in Las Vegas, Nevada.

DEER BLOOD ▶ South Korean international soccer player Park Ji-Sung was such a frail youngster that his parents boosted his strength by feeding him a dish of boiled frogs, antlers, and deer blood. He says it smelled like intestines and tasted so vile that he would sometimes throw up after eating it, but the weird menu worked wonders and eventually earned him a place playing for Manchester United.

OVERSIZE OMELET ▶ 150 chefs in Santarém, Portugal, teamed up to cook a giant omelet that weighed a massive 14,225 lb (6,466 kg)—that's more than 7 tons. The omelet used 145,000 eggs—equal to the weekly yield from 9,000 chickens—880 lb (400 kg) of oil, and 220 lb (100 kg) of butter. It took six hours to cook the omelet in a huge special pan that measured over 32 ft (10 m).

LOCAL GRUB

▶ Mopane worms are a traditional delicacy in southern Africa as, ounce for ounce, they contain more protein than roast chicken breast. The worms, which are really caterpillars, are usually fried with tomatoes, garlic, and onions, but they don't taste much better than they look. People say they are very chewy, difficult to swallow, and taste like a combination of earth, salt, and dry wall!

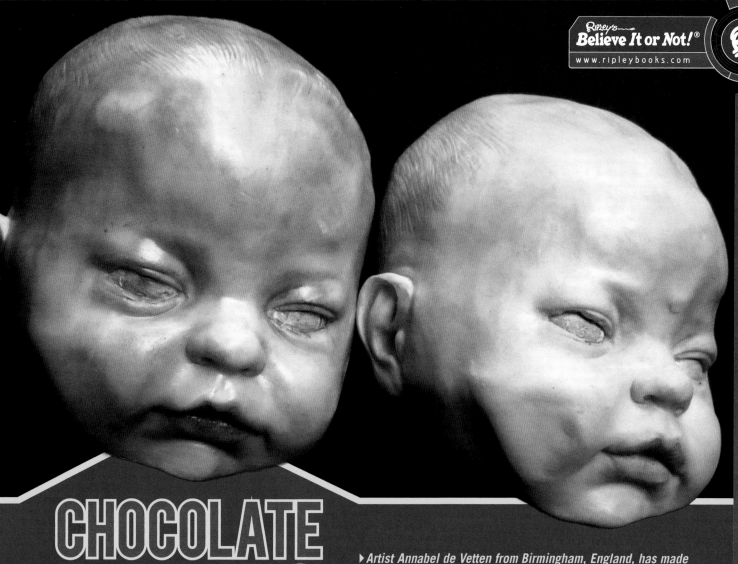

CHOCOLATE BABIES

▶ *Artist Annabel de Vetten from Birmingham, England, has made these disturbingly realistic, life-sized babies' heads out of solid white chocolate. The bizarre, zombie-like heads each weigh nearly 2.2 lb (1 kg), contain 5,000 calories, and sell for £35 ($55). De Vetten, who calls herself "The Cake Conjurer," as she is also an amateur magician, made the heads using a latex mold after she was commissioned to create something that would shock people.*

CHILD GENIUS▶ Heidi Hankins of Hampshire, England, has the IQ of a genius at just four years of age. The average IQ score for an adult is 100 and a "gifted" individual 130, but the youngster boasts an amazing 159—one behind eminent scientist Stephen Hawking. She could read books for seven-year-olds when she was only two and was accepted into Mensa—the high IQ society—before she had even started school.

KEEPING FIT▶ At age 90, Edna Shepherd attends gym classes in Melbourne, Australia, several times a week, taking part in aerobics, tai chi, and body pump. Her fitness regime also includes aqua classes and ballroom dancing.

LONG TRAIN▶ To promote the 2012 Wedding Fair in Bucharest, Romania, ten seamstresses spent 100 days creating a bridal train that was 1.85 mi (3 km) long! To show off the gown, 17-year-old model Ema Dumitrescu took a ride in a hot-air balloon with the dress train flowing beneath her.

TOO LATE▶ In May 2011, police in Walchum, Germany, arrested a 57-year-old man who tried to rob a bank that had been closed for years. He stormed the bank but was disappointed to discover that it was now a physiotherapist's office.

▶ WE SPEND AN AVERAGE OF 9 YEARS OF OUR LIFE WATCHING TV. ◀

BLIND PHOTOGRAPHER ▶ Tara Miller of Winnipeg, Canada, won a 2011 national photography competition despite being legally blind. When taking pictures outdoors she relies upon brightness and shadow in order to be able to frame a photograph, and when she shoots wildlife she relies upon her exceptional hearing to work out where the birds and other animals are so that she can snap them at the most appropriate moment.

AERIAL DANCERS▶ Project Bandaloop, an aerial dance troupe based in California, performs many of its routines dangling from the sides of buildings and cliffs. Strapped to harnesses and ropes, the dancers have carried out breathtakingly original dance sequences hundreds of feet up in the air at Yosemite Falls, as well as performing at other U.S. and international landmarks, including the New York Stock Exchange in New York City and the Eiffel Tower in Paris, France, and in Italy's Dolomite mountains.

EXPLODING HORSES ▶ The U.S. Department of Agriculture has official, published procedures for blowing up animal carcasses with explosives. To obliterate a 1,100-lb (453-kg) horse, it recommends placing 3 lb (1.36 kg) of explosives under the carcass in four different locations as well as 1 lb (0.45 kg) of explosives in two locations on each leg. Horseshoes should be removed in advance of blowing up the horse's carcass in order to prevent flying debris.

COMPLETELY NUTS!

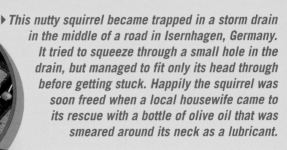

▶ This nutty squirrel became trapped in a storm drain in the middle of a road in Isernhagen, Germany. It tried to squeeze through a small hole in the drain, but managed to fit only its head through before getting stuck. Happily the squirrel was soon freed when a local housewife came to its rescue with a bottle of olive oil that was smeared around its neck as a lubricant.

FAMILIAR FACE▶ Brazilian police charged a man in Recife with using false documents and forgery after he tried to open a bank account using an identification document bearing a photograph of Hollywood actor Jack Nicholson.

BUNGLING BANDITS▶ Two would-be robbers called a bank in Fairfield, Connecticut, on the phone and threatened to create a "blood bath" if a bag of cash was not waiting for them when they arrived. They showed up ten minutes later and seemed surprised that police officers, alerted by the bank, were waiting to arrest them.

DISSOLVED CORPSES▶ As a green alternative to cremation, a funeral home in St. Petersburg, Florida, has installed a unit that works by dissolving the corpse in heated alkaline water. The makers say the process produces one-third less greenhouse gas than cremation and uses one-seventh of the energy.

LOST IN POST▶ Hu Seng from Chongqing, China, paid a courier to deliver him in a sealed box to his girlfriend Li Wang, but the joke backfired when the courier got lost and instead of spending 30 minutes in the box, Hu was trapped for nearly three hours. By the time the package was finally delivered to his girlfriend's office, he had passed out and had to be revived by paramedics. He said ruefully: "I tried to make a hole in the cardboard but it was too thick and I didn't want to spoil the surprise by shouting."

IDENTITY CRISIS▶ A Luciano Pavarotti impersonator for 20 years, Colin Miller from Staffordshire, England, was denied a personalized debit card because his bank refused to accept that his photo was not the real Italian opera singer.

TREE TRAUMA▶ Firefighters in Orange County, California, took 90 minutes to free a man who was stuck up to his chest inside a hollow tree trunk that extended some 5 ft (1.5 m) underground. Sheriff's deputies had located the trapped man by following the sounds of his screams down into a creek bed.

TRAPPED KITTEN▶ A team of five rescuers worked continuously for two days to save a wet and hungry kitten that had become trapped in a 6-in-wide (15-cm) concrete tube beneath a supermarket in Gothcnburg, Sweden.

MOWER SNATCH▶ When keepers at the Australian Reptile Park in Gosford, New South Wales, went into the enclosure of Elvis, a 16-ft (5-m) saltwater crocodile, the aggressive reptile grabbed one of their lawn mowers, dragged it into his pond, and lay at the bottom guarding it.

FLYING VISIT▶ Adventure enthusiasts Grant Engler and Amanda Volf made a spectacular entrance to their beach wedding at Newport Beach, California, by flying into the ceremony wearing water-powered jet packs, each connected by a 30-ft (9-m) hose to a boat. The bride landed on the beach aisle wearing a surfing vest, shorts, and a veil, while the groom wore a white bow tie over a black wetsuit. After exchanging their vows, the couple performed the traditional first dance in midair above the ocean.

BRIDAL RACE▶ One hundred prospective brides donned wedding dresses and running shoes to take part in a 150-meter race in Belgrade, Serbia, with the winner earning a free wedding.

OSTRICH ATTACK▶ In Hastings, New Zealand, Phillip Russell was jailed for six months for assaulting his wife with an ostrich egg. He threw the huge egg at her, bruising her chest, after losing his temper because her pet pig had damaged his power saw.

SEEING DOUBLE

▶ When student Max Galuppo of Bloomsbury, New Jersey, visited the Philadelphia Museum of Art, he was stunned to see his doppelganger in *Portrait of a Nobleman with Dueling Gauntlet*, a 16th-century picture by an unknown artist. However, the resemblance may not be entirely coincidental as Max's grandparents come from the same area of northern Italy where the portrait is believed to have been painted.

THAT'S QUACKERS!

▶Wayne Algenio won a New York City speed-eating competition by having the stomach to devour 18 balut—boiled fertilized duck fetuses complete with beak, soft bones, and moist feathers—in five minutes. A high-protein Filipino delicacy, balut is eaten in its shell and is usually dipped in salt and washed down with beer.

CREEPY RECIPES▶ A 2012 Dutch book, *The Insect Cookbook*, suggests dozens of ways of incorporating insects into everyday meals, such as adding worms to chocolate muffins and grasshoppers to a mushroom risotto.

CUPCAKE CROWN▶ On April 14, 2012, at the Isle Waterloo World Cupcake Eating Championship in Iowa, Patrick "Deep Dish" Bertoletti ate a world record 72 cupcakes in just six minutes.

VOLCANIC GRILL▶ The staff of the El Diablo restaurant, on the island of Lanzarote in the Canary Islands, Spain, cook food over the heat of an active volcano. A giant grill over the volcanic vent enables them to cook meat and fish dishes at temperatures of between 840°F (450°C) and 930°F (500°C).

LUCKY LEG▶ A bullfrog was saved from being made into soup in Zhuzhou, China, when a chef spotted that it had a fifth leg. Instead of being eaten, the freaky frog was sent to a zoo.

COOKIE TOWER▶ On March 16, 2012, students at Woodrush High School, Worcestershire, England, made a cookie tower more than 6 ft (1.8 m) high from 11,500 cookies.

FAVORITE DRINK▶ Claire Ayton from Warwickshire, England, drank 8.4 pt (4 l) of Diet Coke every day for ten years. In total, that's 30,855 pt (14,600 l) at a cost of nearly $20,000. She also gained 42 lb (19 kg) in weight.

CARNIVOROUS COCKTAIL▶ The Ruby Lo bar in London, England, used to serve "True" Bloody Marys—alcohol mixed with pasteurized blood.

CAKE CAR▶ Carey Iennaccaro and Mike Elder built a 95-percent cake car that reached a speed of 28 mph (45 km/h) in Kansas City, Missouri, on March 4, 2012—the world's fastest cake car. The 716-lb (325-kg) car was edible except for the tires, aluminum chassis, and brakes. At the wheel, Iennaccaro wore a chocolate helmet and sat on a cake cushion watching a frosting speedometer!

GOAT DROPPINGS▶ Argan oil, a popular delicacy in Morocco, where it is used for dipping bread and to flavor couscous and salad dressings, is collected from the droppings of native Tamri goats. After the goats have feasted on the fruits of the argan tree, they leave behind the hard nuts in their droppings. The droppings are then collected by local women and sifted to remove the kernels, which are ground up to produce the valuable oil.

BEER SPILL▶ A truck crashed in Sachsen Anhalt, Germany, spilling 27 tons of beer crates and sending beer flowing for several hundred yards down the autobahn. Firemen, wearing breathing apparatus to protect them from the beer fumes, had to close the road for several hours.

MINE HOST▶ Muru, a restaurant near Helsinki, Finland, offers customers the chance to dine 262 ft (80 m) underground in the Tytyri Mine Museum. Diners wear safety helmets for the descent and during their meal can go down an additional 1,150 ft (350 m) via an elevator shaft.

OLDEST GROOM ▶ Hazi Abdul Noor, officially registered as 116 years old but who claimed to be 120, married 60-year-old Samoi Bibi in front of 500 guests at a ceremony in Satghari, India, in 2011. He is head of a family of 122, including two sons, four daughters, and a lot of grandchildren.

MINE CLEARER ▶ Aki Ra, once a child soldier in Cambodia, digs up and defuses land mines, and he started out by using only a knife and a sharp stick. He and his team now use more sophisticated equipment and have cleared over 50,000 devices.

HAPPY ANNIVERSARY ▶ British Army Lance Corporal Scott Townson saved the life of fellow soldier Lance Corporal Craig Turley twice in a year—and both incidents occurred on September 23! First, Lance Corporal Turley was on patrol in Afghanistan when an exploding grenade nearly blew off his left hand and severed an artery, and then exactly a year later he was bitten by a venomous Egyptian cobra while training in Kenya. On both occasions Lance Corporal Townson, an army medic, was on hand to save his friend.

NUMBER SEQUENCE ▶ Laila Fitzgerald of Des Moines, Iowa, was born weighing 8 lb 9 oz on October 11, 2012, at 1.14 p.m., giving her a numerical sequence of 8-9-10-11-12-13-14.

ZOMBIFY YOURSELF ▶ People who think their wedding photos are a bit bland can now have them "zombified!" Rob Sacchetto from Sudbury, Ontario, runs zombieportraits.com, which offers people the chance to have their photos customized with hand-painted artwork that turns them into crazed zombies. He has also used ink and watercolor to zombify photos of the likes of Donald Trump, Kanye West, Alfred Hitchcock, and Lindsay Lohan.

DESIGNER MONKEY

▶ Wearing a tiny shearling coat and a diaper, this seven-month-old Japanese macaque monkey was spotted wandering around the parking lot of an Ikea store in Toronto, Canada. The monkey, named Darwin, had escaped from a crate in his owner's car.

MISSING MILLIONS ▶ A bumper $96-million Lottery Euromillions jackpot went unclaimed in December 2012 because the mystery winning ticketholder from Hertfordshire, England, missed the 180-day deadline to make a claim.

DOG CALL ▶ After receiving a mysterious silent call on his cell phone from the phone in his empty house, Bruce Gardner of Orem, Utah, immediately rang the police to report that his house was being broken into—only to discover later that the "call" had come from his pet Labrador Maya. The dog had got hold of his cordless home phone and while chewing it, had happened to hit redial.

PENNY PILE ▶ Thomas Daigle of Milford, Massachusetts, paid off the final bill of his house mortgage entirely in pennies—62,000 of them! He meticulously collected pennies for 35 years until he had 400 lb (182 kg) of rolled-up coins, which he took to the loans company in two heavy steel boxes. It took the bank two days to count the coins and verify that the mortgage was paid.

PARALLEL LIVES ▶ Emilie Falk and Lin Backman, nonidentical twins born in Semarang, Indonesia, in 1983, were separately adopted by Swedish parents, but reunited 29 years later after discovering they lived only 25 mi (40 km) apart. Although raised independently, both became teachers, they got married on the same day just one year apart, and they even danced to the same wedding song, "You and Me" by Lifehouse.

CAN SCULPTURE ▶ Volunteers in Abu Dhabi, U.A.E., took six days to build an enormous aluminum can sculpture from 46,556 cans. The model of the 200-year-old Al Maqta'a Fort stood 18.6 ft (5.7 m) high and measured 13 ft (4 m) wide at the base. It was stuck together using 919 bottles of superglue and 521 cans of liquid nail glue.

DEAD BEES ▶ Matthew Brandt from Los Angeles, California, created an image of a bee, composed entirely from the crumbled parts of dead bees. He acquired his natural materials after discovering hundreds of dead honeybees scattered along the Californian shoreline.

OLD WIVES' SALES ▶ Until 1857, it was legal for British husbands to sell their wives. The going rate was £3,000 ($4,550), the equivalent in today's money of about £220,000 ($335,000).

SHARP END ▶

▶ *Shaolin monks balance their bodies on the tips of sharp spears in a demonstration of the Chinese martial art Qigong during the opening ceremony of the Fourth Southern Shaolin Martial Arts Cultural Festival in Putian. Qigong teaches the body to relax so that no pain is felt.*

HEAD IN A BOOK

▶ *Artist Maskull Lasserre from Montreal, Canada, carved an intricate replica of a human skull from seven thick software manuals. Using an angle grinder and router, and working in short bursts of between 20 and 60 minutes at a time, it took him over 200 hours to complete the sculpture. He has also carved an impressive likeness of a human rib cage from a stack of old newspapers.*

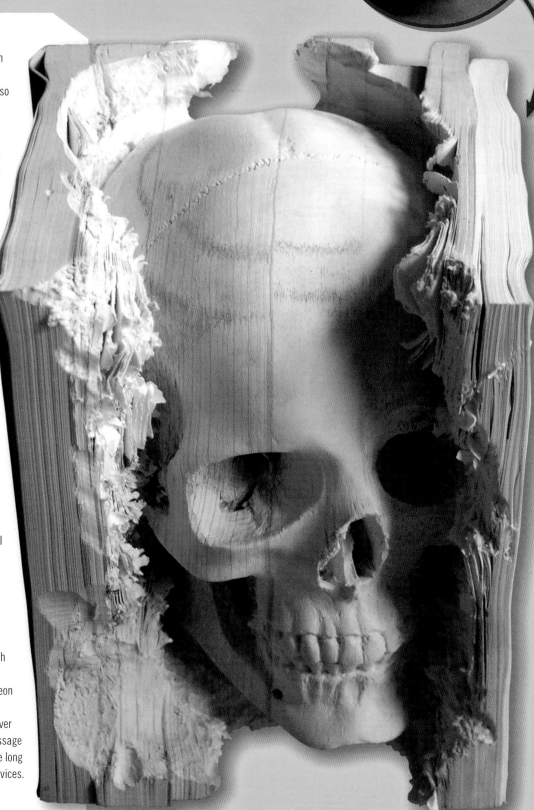

LEAP DAY▶ Michelle Birnbaum of Saddle River, New Jersey, was born on February 29, 1980, and in 2008, amazingly, her daughter Rose was also born on February 29—leap day.

UNDERWATER WEDDING▶ More than 200 SCUBA divers attended the July 17, 2011, underwater wedding of Alberto dal Lago and Karla Munguia, which took place 16 ft (5 m) deep in the ocean off the coast of Playa Del Carmen, Mexico. The civil judge, who wed them, and his secretary both had to learn to SCUBA dive in order to conduct the ceremony.

CLOSE SHAVE▶ A 57-year-old man who had fallen asleep in a cornfield on the outskirts of Billings, Montana, had a miraculous escape when he was run over by a large combine harvester. The man's clothing was sucked into the cutter and he was trapped in the blades, but survived with just cuts and bruises.

PIGEON MESSAGE▶ A carrier pigeon dispatched during World War II to relay a secret message, possibly about the D-Day landings, was found around 70 years later in the chimney of a house in Surrey, England—its communiqué still attached to its skeleton in a red capsule. Some 250,000 birds were used by the British military and emergency services in World War II, to form the National Pigeon Service, 32 of which received medals for distinguished service. This one never reached its destination—and its message is so secret that it is written in a code long since forgotten by British security services.

BREAKING THE MOLD

▶ Estonian artist Heikki Leis takes close-up photographs of fruit and vegetables, which have been left to rot for months, to create images of weird sci-fi creatures and spectacular landscapes. Among his artworks are a moldy rutabaga (right) that resembles a hydrogen-bomb mushroom cloud and a rotten beet that looks like an alien monster (below).

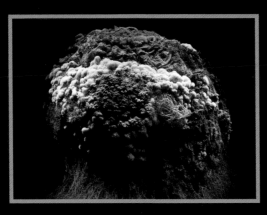

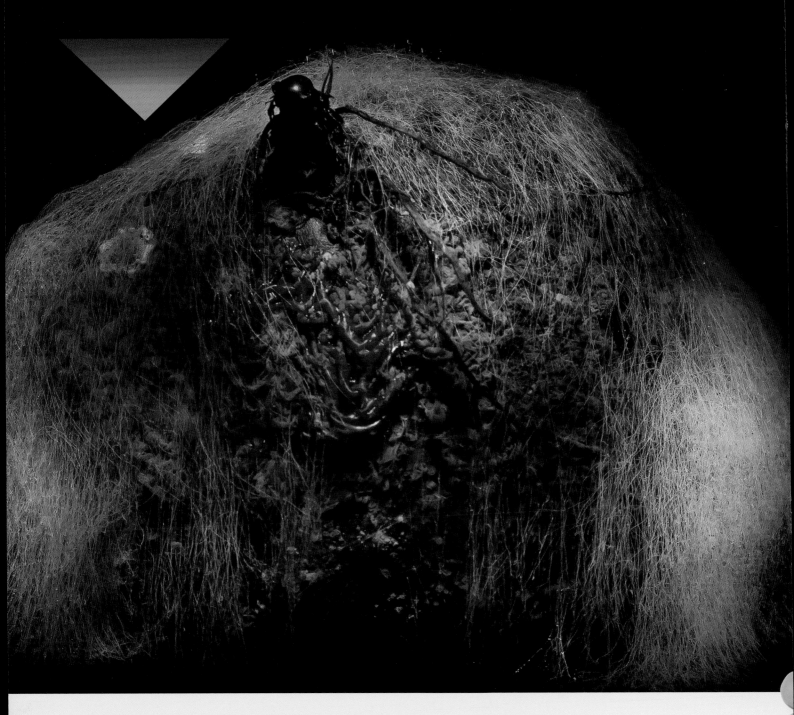

LONG LOG ▶ Eighty chefs at the Pudong Shangri-La Hotel in Shanghai, China, created a 3,503-ft-long (1,068-m), vanilla-flavored Yule log cake. Made using 904 eggs over a period of 24 hours, the giant cake was set out on 156 tables.

GRAVEYARD DINER ▶ The Lucky Hotel restaurant in Ahmedabad, India, was built in the 1960s over a graveyard—and today customers drink tea at tables next to 22 tombs set in the floor. Waiters jump over the green tombs to serve food, but these are not the restaurant's only unusual features—a large tree runs through the middle of the dining room and extends out through the roof.

PEDIGREE DOG ▶ On May 31, 2012, Mike Brown, the owner of Capitol Dawg in Sacramento, California, created a very expensive hot dog— the $145.49 luxury dog. It featured an 18-in (45-cm), 12-oz (340-g) all-beef frankfurter, expensive and rare moose cheese from Sweden, white truffle butter, whole grain mustard from France, and New Hampshire bacon marinated in maple syrup.

GREEN HONEY ▶ Bees at apiaries in Ribeauville, France, have been producing green and blue honey! The unusual coloring is thought to have been caused by the bees eating the sugary residue from containers of M&M's® candy that were being processed at a nearby biogas plant. Unfortunately, the honey was not considered sellable.

BUG PIZZA

▶ Taiwanese water bugs, joro spiders, caterpillar moths, and larvae were the interesting insect toppings served on a pizza at a bug-eating party in Tokyo, Japan. While insects are a good source of protein, eating them has traditionally been associated with people who couldn't afford to buy animal meat. However, bug eating is steadily growing in popularity as more and more people look to sustainable food sources in our over-populated world.

MAYO LOVER ▶ Philippa Garfield of London, England, loves mayo so much she eats it on sandwiches, on cookies, on fruit—and even puts it in her tea instead of using milk. Not content with that, she washes her hair with mayo and also uses it as face cream!

▶ FLAMINGO TONGUE AND ROAST PARROT WERE POPULAR DELICACIES AT ROMAN FEASTS. ◀

TITANIC FEAST ▶ A restaurant in Houston, Texas, commemorated the 100th anniversary of the *Titanic* sinking on April 14, 2012, by offering a re-creation of the last meal served to the ship's first-class passengers for a price of $1,000 per person.

PRICEY PIZZA ▶ The Steveston Pizza Company in Vancouver, Canada, created a $450 pizza, made with lobster thermidor, Alaskan black cod, and a side of Russian osetra caviar.

CHESTNUT CHAMP ▶ On March 17, 2012, at the TooJay's World Class Corned Beef Eating Championship in Palm Beach Gardens, Florida, Joey "Jaws" Chestnut from San Jose, California, won by devouring 20 corned-beef sandwiches— each weighing 8 oz (225 g)—in just ten minutes. Also in 2012, he consumed 390 shrimp wantons in eight minutes at the finale of the CP Biggest Eater Competition in Bangkok, Thailand.

MONSTER PIE ▶ In Moscow, Russia, chefs used hundreds of pounds of flour, berries, and sugar plus 500 eggs to make a gigantic blueberry pie weighing 660 lb (300 kg) and measuring 230 ft (70 m) long.

PICNIC PARTY ▶ On July 15, 2012, in Kitchener, Ontario, some 5,000 people ate their lunch on more than 1,000 picnic tables, which stretched along the street for almost 1½ mi (2.3 km).

METEORITE WINE ▶ A vineyard in San Vicente, Chile, owned by British-born Ian Hutcheon, has launched 2010 Meteorito, a Cabernet Sauvignon wine infused with a 4.5-billion-year-old meteorite. The wine has been fermented for 12 months in a barrel containing the 3-in (7.5-cm) meteorite, which Hutcheon, a keen astronomer and winemaker, loaned from an American collector.

MINI NUN

▶ Worshipers at a temple in Haridwar, India, bow at the feet of Anjali Barma, a nun who is just 2 ft 7 in (78.8 cm) tall. The 65-year-old, who is also known as Ganga Maa, says visitors think she is an extra-special holy woman because of her stature. However, when she was just ten years old, her lack of inches led to her being kidnapped by a circus owner who held her captive for several months and tried in vain to persuade her to perform on stage as a human oddity.

SPACE ART

▶ Josh Taylor from Surrey, England, created a unique piece of space art at an altitude of 100,000 ft (30,500 m) using a helium weather balloon. Containing tubes of green, blue, brown, and yellow paint to represent the earth, sea, desert, and sun, the balloon was launched into the sky over Worcestershire and during the ascent the colors were slowly released from the tubes onto a canvas. When the balloon reached 100,810 ft (30,725 m), it burst and plummeted back down to the ground where the artwork was located by means of a tracking device.

CAT BURGLAR ▶ A trap set up to catch an office thief at an animal shelter in Swinoujscie, Poland, caught a real-life cat burglar. The secret camera captured a two-year-old Burmese cat named Clement sneaking into the office at midnight, stealing the cash, and hiding it under a sofa. Her nighttime raids had netted her more than $300 in a month.

MISTAKEN IDENTITY ▶ In October 2011, a lifeboat and a helicopter from Tyneside, England, were sent on an emergency North Sea rescue mission after a member of the public mistook the planet Jupiter for a distress flare. Jupiter is particularly low in the sky at that time of year and also gives off a bright red light that can be mistaken for flares.

SQUID-BOT ▶ Scientists at Harvard University, United States, have devised a rubbery, squidlike robot, which can crawl and camouflage itself, made from soft, sheer polymers. Based on sea creatures that can control their appearance, the robot has a thin sheet of special silicone with tiny channels through which colored liquids are pumped so that its skin mimics its surroundings.

OLDEST MESSAGE ▶ Fishing off the Shetland Islands in August 2012, Scottish boat skipper Andrew Leaper discovered a message in a bottle dated June 1914, making it, at 98 years old, the oldest message in a bottle ever found. Amazingly, the previous record-holding bottle—a 93-year-old message found in 2006—was picked up in the same area by the same fishing boat, the *Copious*.

MODEL BABIES

▶ *Parents can now hold their baby before it is born—thanks to a technique that uses a 3-D printer to transform an ultrasound scan into an anatomically correct resin replica of the fetus. The models—marketed by Japanese company FASOTEC and costing over $1,000 each—come in a standard size of 3½ in (9 cm), but are also available in miniature so that proud parents can dangle their babies from a key chain.*

GETAWAY FARE▶ A would-be bank robber was arrested in Chamblee, Georgia, after returning to the scene of his crime to withdraw money for his cab fare. Fleeing empty-handed from the bank, the gunman jumped into a cab to ride to his getaway car, only to realize he had no money for the fare. So he returned to the same bank to withdraw cash legally, but was recognized by staff.

HOT LINE▶ Solenne San Jose, from Pessac, France, was horrified to receive a telephone bill for $14,766,481,895,641,556—the equivalent of nearly 6,000 times France's annual economic output. The bill should have been for around $100.

CRIME PAYS▶ An Austrian court ordered bank robber Otto Neuman to be given back $82,000 that he stole 19 years earlier because neither the bank nor its insurers wanted the money. After getting into financial difficulties, bank manager Neuman recruited two friends to help him snatch $240,000 in cash and gold bars from his branch in Vienna. By the time Neuman was apprehended and jailed, $158,000 had been spent. However, the bank was insured for the robbery and the insurance company made its money back on the rising value of the gold bars.

BARGAIN RATE▶ Isidore and Joan Schwartz stayed at the Waldorf-Astoria Hotel in New York City, on their wedding night in 1952. When they returned in 2012 for their 60th wedding anniversary, they paid the same price as their first visit—$16.80, even though rooms at the hotel now start at $319 a night.

MAGIC NUMBER▶ Kiam Moriya from Birmingham, Alabama, was born on December 12, 2000 at 12 minutes after midday, meaning that he turned 12 on 12/12/12 at 12.12 p.m.

HOT LIPS

▶ To attract pollinating butterflies and hummingbirds, the small white flowers of the shrub *Psychotria elata* are surrounded by large red leaves that look like a pair of luscious lips. No wonder the plant, which is found in Central America, is sometimes known as "Mick Jagger's lips"!

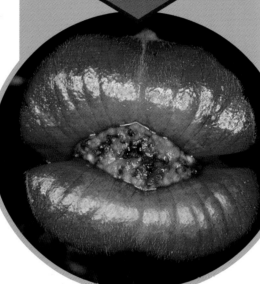

METEOR BLAST▶ A meteor measuring more than 55 ft (17 m) wide and weighing 10,000 tons entered the Earth's atmosphere at a speed of 40,000 mph (64,000 km/h) on February 15, 2013, before exploding some 15 mi (24 km) above ground with a force 33 times more powerful than the atomic bomb that destroyed Hiroshima in 1945. The largest space rock strike to hit Earth for over a century, it blew in around a million square feet (93,000 m²) of glass in the Russian city of Chelyabinsk, damaged 3,000 buildings, and created a 50-ft (15-m) hole in a frozen lake. The meteor left a trail in the sky that was 300 mi (480 km) long. The shockwave from the Russian explosion was detected by sensors halfway around the world—as far afield as Africa and Greenland.

WEDDING-DAY FALL▶ Derek and Cassy McBride of Erie, Pennsylvania, were married in a hospital chapel after the groom suffered a collapsed lung and broke three ribs when he fell down a flight of stairs earlier on the day of their wedding—June 25, 2011.

SLEEPY DRIVER▶ A Swiss driver whose car veered off the road, down an embankment, and plunged into a stream after he had dozed off at the wheel was still fast asleep when rescuers pulled him out. Medics thought 49-year-old Manfred Hofer, from Willisau, Switzerland, was unconscious but in fact he was just in a deep sleep.

TEENAGE TRANCE▶ Several teenaged students attending an end-of-term hypnosis show at a private girls' high school in Sherbrooke, Canada, became stuck in a trance, forcing the young hypnotist to summon his mentor to snap them back into reality. The girls remained in the spell cast by 20-year-old Maxime Nadeau for several hours until his mentor, Richard Whitbread, arrived.

ROPE JUMPING

▶ In their search for new thrills, more than 3,000 young Russians have taken up the extreme sport of rope jumping, leaping from a mountain or bridge and plunging hundreds of feet through the air tied to a homemade rope. Unlike a bungee cord, the rope does not have an elastic slack, so jumpers must try to form an arc shape with it so that it cushions their fall. For an added twist, some of the youngsters have started performing the daredevil jumps on snowboards.

BURGER
MUMMY

▶ *This 5-ft-2-in-tall (1.57-m) mummified skeleton was made by Texas artist Ben Campbell from $200 of ground-up burgers and French fries! After drying the food out, he ran it through a blender, mixed it with adhesive resin, and then packed it into rubber molds before bonding together the cast pieces. He says: "As long as it is kept dry, it should last for thousands of years, like a real mummy."*

TESTING DAY ▶ Emma French of Livingston, Scotland, took her driving test while she was in labor—and managed to pass despite having four contractions during the test. Immediately afterward, she drove herself to the hospital and gave birth just hours later.

BRIDGE STOLEN ▶ A 50-ft-long (15-m) metal bridge was stolen in North Beaver Township, Pennsylvania, after thieves used a blowtorch to cut it apart.

BULLET BLOCKER ▶ A storeowner in Savannah, Georgia, was shot during an armed robbery but suffered only a minor cut when the medallions hanging around his neck deflected the bullet.

MAGIC NUMBER ▶ Twins Race and Brooke Belmont from Tampa, Florida, turned 11 on 11/11/11 (November 11, 2011).

ATE BRAIN ▶ Andy Millns of London, England, ate a replica of his own brain, made from chocolate. Experts at a technology company took an MRI scan of his head, fed a map of his brain into a computer, and printed it out on a 3-D printer. A latex mold of the brain was then created and filled with liquid chocolate.

MOLECULAR MOTOR ▶ Researchers from Tufts University of Medford, Massachusetts, created an electric motor built from a single molecule that is 300 times smaller than the width of a human hair.

CHOCOLATE TEMPLE ▶ In May 2012, staff at Qzina Specialty Foods in Irvine, California, made the world's biggest chocolate sculpture—a replica model of an ancient Mayan temple weighing 18,239 lb (8,280 kg). It took 400 hours to build and the finished product stood 6 ft (1.8 m) tall with a 10 x 10 ft (3 x 3 m) base.

KILLER CURRIES ▶ A curry-eating competition in Edinburgh, Scotland, on October 1, 2011, featured curry so hot that contestants started vomiting, fainting, and writhing on the floor in agony. One participant was so ill after sampling the "Kismot Killer" that she was rushed to a hospital twice in a matter of hours.

THE HONEYMOO-NERS ▶ Beef farmer Michael Hanson and his bride Hayley Morgan arrived at their bovine-themed wedding on a tractor and their wedding photos were posed in a muddy field alongside a herd of cattle in Llandefalle, Wales. They spent their honeymoon in Texas, touring cattle farms.

GOOD SAMARITAN ▶ When Gerald Gronowski had a flat tire near Cleveland, Ohio, a man named Christopher Manacci stopped to help. As they talked, Gronowski realized that Manacci was the same kindly stranger who had helped him extract a fishing hook from his wounded hand eight years earlier.

FAN MAN ▶ Eighty-two-year-old M. Natarajan, a Hindu devotee from Madurai, Tamil Nadu, India, has spent every day of the past 52 years fanning the visitors of local temples to keep them cool. In that time he has worn through five 6.6-lb (3-kg) peacock fans.

ILLEGIBLE NOTE ▶ A bank robbery was foiled in New Castle, Delaware, when the bank teller was unable to read the illegible handwriting on the robber's note.

STRONG MATERIAL ▶ Graphene, a material made from molecular sheets of carbon, is hundreds of times stronger than steel. It would take the weight of an elephant balanced on a pencil to penetrate a sheet as thin as household plastic wrap.

GUIDED BULLET ▶ Researchers in Albuquerque, New Mexico, have invented a prototype bullet that can steer itself in mid-flight. The bullet uses tiny fins to correct the course of its flight, which enable it to hit laser-lit targets at distances of about 1¼ mi (2 km).

SUSPICIOUS PACKAGES ▶ Two men trying to board an airplane at Indira Gandhi International Airport in Delhi, India, tried to conceal live small mammals in their underpants. Suspicious customs officers discovered that the men, en route from Dubai, U.A.E., to Bangkok, Thailand, had slender lorises concealed in pouches in their briefs.

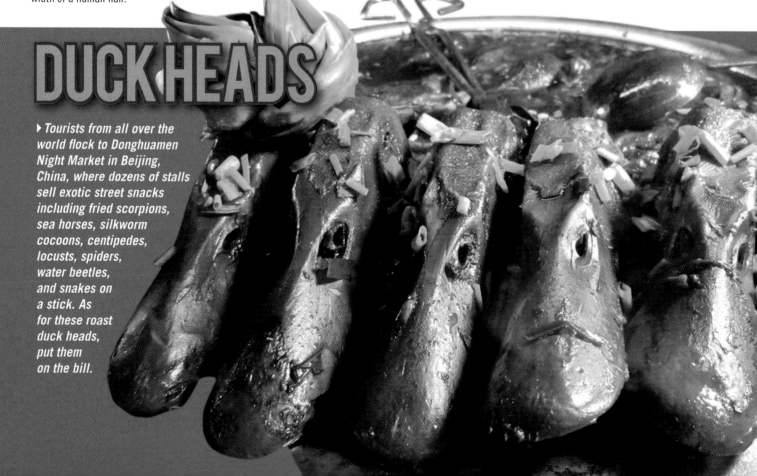

DUCK HEADS

▶ Tourists from all over the world flock to Donghuamen Night Market in Beijing, China, where dozens of stalls sell exotic street snacks including fried scorpions, sea horses, silkworm cocoons, centipedes, locusts, spiders, water beetles, and snakes on a stick. As for these roast duck heads, put them on the bill.

SOLEMATES

The world's smallest woman, Jyoti Amge, met the second tallest man, Brahim Takioullah, in March 2013, and discovered his feet are four times bigger than hers!

Nineteen-year-old Jyoti, who was also featured in *Ripley's Believe It or Not! Enter If You Dare!* in 2011, stands at 24.7 in (62.8 cm) while thirty-one-year-old Brahim measures over 8 ft (246 cm) in height. Brahim's feet also dwarfed Jyoti's feet, measuring a massive 1 ft 3 in (38.1 cm)—Jyoti's are just 3.72 in (9.46 cm) in length—as the biggest feet in the world.

SWEET SNAKE

▶ U.S. company Vat19 has created an edible gummi python that measures 8 ft (2.4 m) long and weighs 27 lb (12.2 kg). Selling for nearly $150, the monster snake boasts scary eyes, blended colors, ridged coils, thousands of individually carved scales, and comes in blue raspberry flavor with either green apple or red cherry sections. The Party Python contains a whopping 36,000 calories—18 times an adult's recommended daily allowance.

DELAYED PICTURES▶ A centenarian couple from Nanchong, China, finally posed for their wedding photos in 2012—88 years after getting married. When Wu Conghan, 101, and his wife Wu Songshi, 103, married back in 1924, they did not have the option of wedding photos.

MOO-TON CADET▶ In an attempt to produce the best beef in Europe, some farmers in southern France give their cows a daily feed of up to two bottles of fine wine, mixed in with barley and hay.

COFFEE BLAST▶ Over 1,000 baristas gathered in the main square at Zagreb, Croatia, to operate 22 coffee machines and, in just over three hours, fill a giant coffee cup with 4,252 pt (2,012 l) of cappuccino—the largest ever cappuccino coffee.

DOG GONE▶ In 2012, Joey Chestnut won his sixth straight Nathan's 4th of July Hot Dog Eating Contest at Coney Island, New York. He devoured 68 dogs and buns in ten minutes, beating his closest rival by an impressive 16 dogs!

KING KEBAB▶ In June 2012, cooks in Ankara, Turkey, created the world's biggest kebab—a 2,641-lb (1,198-kg) monster made from the meat of seven cows. The kebab stood over 8 ft (2.5 m) tall and needed a crane to haul it into place. The ten cooks had to work on scaffolding to prepare it.

CRACK COOK▶ Correy Peras, a cook from Ottowa, Ontario, Canada, cracked an incredible 3,031 eggs in an hour using only one hand on June 22, 2012.

WEDDING RECORD▶ An amazing 95 bridesmaids attended the wedding of Keyoon Chokelamlert and Kriangkrai Kittithanesuan in Thailand in 2012, breaking a world record.

SLICE OF LUCK▶ When Liz Douglas of Stirling, Scotland, was involved in a serious car crash, her life was saved by a loaf of bread. The medium-sliced loaf fell from her shopping bag and cushioned her head when her car plowed into a telephone pole, allowing her to escape with only minor cuts and bruises.

SKELETON FIND▶ Police officers in Lille, France, found the skeleton of a man who had been lying undiscovered in bed for 16 years. Unopened mail at the derelict house dated back to 1996.

SISTER SEARCH▶ Separated from her twin sister at birth, Jennifer Wilson, from Rotherham, South Yorkshire, England, spent 55 years searching for her sibling, Kathleen Millns, only to find that she had always lived just 3 miles (4.8km) away in the same town. The two women even shared the same doctor and dentist.

GETAWAY DONKEY▶ Three Colombian crooks who raided a convenience store had to abandon their loot because their getaway donkey made too much noise and alerted the police. After snatching foodstuffs from the store in Juan de Acosta, the robbers loaded them onto ten-year-old Xavi, a donkey they had stolen earlier in the day, but the animal then started braying loudly, causing them to ditch the donkey and make their escape on foot.

BONE IDOL

▶ *U.K. butcher Anthony Dunphy has turned his work into an art form by using meat in his paintings! He combines gloss paint with lamb and chicken bones to create 4-ft-high (1.2-m) artworks—such as this portrait of Amy Winehouse—which he says are inspired by pop art pioneer Andy Warhol.*

▲ Anthony also created a portrait of David Beckham especially for Ripley's from meat and bones.

RAISED BY MONKEYS▶ Marina Chapman, a housewife from Bradford, West Yorkshire, England, spent five years as a child in the 1950s being raised by monkeys in the Colombian jungle. After being kidnapped at the age of five, she was abandoned in the jungle where she lived a Tarzan-like existence with a colony of capuchin monkeys and learned to catch birds and rabbits with her bare hands. Monkeys are known to accept young humans into their group—a four-year-old Ugandan boy, John Ssebunya, lived for more than a year with vervet monkeys in the jungle before being rescued and adapting well to life with people.

LUCKY CORNER▶ In the space of five years, three neighbors living within 164 ft (50 m) of each other in Miramichi, New Brunswick, Canada, each won cars in separate contests. In 2004, the parents of Dana MacDonald won a new Pontiac Sunfire, in 2007, her neighbor won a Pontiac Solstice, and in 2009 she and her boyfriend won a Chevrolet Silverado truck in another contest.

DIED TWICE▶ Two-year-old Kelvin Santos, of Belem, Brazil, was pronounced dead on June 1, 2012 and during his wake the next day, he sat up in his coffin, requested a drink of water, then laid down again and was once more confirmed dead.

INDEX

ACKNOWLEDGMENTS

Cover (r) Maskull Lasserre, (l) © PA/Police Grossburgwedel; **4** Annabel de Vetten; **6** (t/l) David Begiashvili, (b) Getty Images; **7** Startraks Photo/Rex Features; **8** Circus World Museum, Baraboo, Wisconsin; **9** (t) Hernandez Silva arquitectura/Rex Features, (b) Steve Rosenow/Loowit Imaging; **10** (t) © Rungroj Yongrit/epa/Corbis; **11** Jaffa Cakes/Rex Features; **12** (t) Steve Grubman, (b) © Michele Westmorland/Corbis; **13** www.corsozundert.nl/Rex Features; **14** Caters News; **15** (t) Bournemouth News/Rex Features, (b) Dominic Deville; **16** (t) Jack Dempsey/Invision for Cheetos/AP Images, (b) KNS News; **17** (t) Joshua Scott, (b) Caters News; **18** Logan Cooper; **19** Annabel de Vetten; **20** (b) Nikkie Curtis/Max Galuppo, (t) © PA/Police Grossburgwedel; **21** Reuters/Keith Bedford; **22** (t) Lisa Lin/Rex Features, (b) Reuters/China Daily; **23** Maskull Lasserre; **24** (b) Richard Jones/Sinopix/Rex Features, (t) Caters News; **25** (t/l, t/r) Caters News, (b) Reuters/Vincent Kessler, (b/l) © Liaurinko - Fotolia.com; **26** Cover Asia Press; **27** (t) Caters News, (b) Yoshikazu Tsuno/AFP/Getty Images; **28** (t) Sell Your Photo, (b) Dr Morley Read/Science Photo Library; **29** WENN.com; **30** Melinda Chan; **31** Rex; **32** (t) Vat19.com/Rex Features; **33** (c) Caters News, (b/r) Anthony Dunphy, artist, anthonyartwork@hotmail.co.uk/Nick Morgan @ ME5H/Cut Media; **Back cover** Melinda Chan

Key: t = top, b = bottom, c = center, l = left, r = right, sp = single page, dp = double page

All other photos are from Ripley Entertainment Inc.
Every attempt has been made to acknowledge correctly and contact copyright holders and we apologize in advance for any unintentional errors or omissions, which will be corrected in future editions.

J
031.02
S

BC#33910049012736 $20.95

Seriously weird!

cly
11/24/14